contents

Mediterranean Fish Soup

Makes 6 servings

PREP TIME
10 minutes

COOK TIME
20 minutes

2 tablespoons olive oil

1 large sweet onion, chopped (about 2 cups)

¼ cup dry white wine *or* Swanson® Chicken Broth

4 cups Swanson® Vegetable Broth *or* Chicken Broth (Regular *or* Certified Organic)

1 can (14.5 ounces) diced tomatoes, undrained

24 mussels, scrubbed and beards removed

1 pound firm white fish fillet (cod, haddock *or* halibut), cut into 1-inch pieces

½ pound fresh *or* thawed frozen large shrimp, peeled and deveined

Shredded fresh basil leaves

Kitchen **Tip**

Select mussels with tightly closed shells or shells that snap shut when lightly tapped. Avoid mussels with broken shells.

1. Heat the oil in a 6-quart saucepot over medium heat. Add the onion and cook until it's tender.

2. Add the wine and cook for 1 minute. Stir in the broth and tomatoes and heat to a boil. Reduce the heat to low. Add the mussels, fish and shrimp. Cover and cook until the mussels open, the fish flakes easily when tested with a fork and the shrimp are cooked through. Discard any mussels that do not open. Season as desired. Garnish with the basil.

West African Vegetable Stew

Makes 6 servings

PREP TIME
15 minutes

COOK TIME
30 minutes

1 tablespoon vegetable oil

2 large onions, sliced (about 2 cups)

2 cloves garlic, minced

1 pound sweet potatoes, peeled, cut in half lengthwise and cut into ¼-inch slices

1 large tomato, coarsely chopped (about 2 cups)

½ cup raisins

½ teaspoon ground cinnamon

½ teaspoon crushed red pepper

1 can (10½ ounces) Campbell's® Condensed Chicken Broth

½ cup water

1 can (about 15 ounces) chickpeas (garbanzo beans), rinsed and drained

4 coarsely chopped fresh spinach leaves

Hot cooked rice *or* couscous

1. Heat the oil in a 12-inch skillet over medium heat. Add the onion and garlic and cook until the onion is tender.

2. Add the potatoes and tomatoes to the skillet and cook for 5 minutes. Stir in the raisins, cinnamon, red pepper, broth and water and heat to a boil. Reduce the heat to low. Cover and cook for 15 minutes or until the potatoes are tender.

3. Stir in the chickpeas and spinach and cook until the spinach is wilted. Serve with the rice, if desired.

Southwest White Chicken Chili

Makes 6 servings

PREP TIME
10 minutes

COOK TIME
20 minutes

1 tablespoon vegetable oil

4 skinless, boneless chicken breast halves (about 1 pound), cut into cubes

4 teaspoons chili powder

2 teaspoons ground cumin

1 large onion, chopped (about 1 cup)

1 medium green pepper, chopped (about ¾ cup)

1 can (10¾ ounces) Campbell's® Condensed Cream of Chicken Soup (Regular *or* 98% Fat Free)

¾ cup water

1½ cups frozen whole kernel corn

2 cans (about 15 ounces *each*) white kidney beans (cannellini), rinsed and drained

2 tablespoons shredded Cheddar cheese

1. Heat the oil in a 4-quart saucepan over medium-high heat. Add the chicken, chili powder, cumin, onion and pepper and cook until the chicken is cooked through and the vegetables are tender, stirring often.

2. Stir the soup, water, corn and beans in the saucepan and heat to a boil. Reduce the heat to low. Cover and cook for 5 minutes, stirring occasionally. Sprinkle with the cheese.

Chili & Rice

Makes 4 servings

PREP TIME
10 minutes

COOK TIME
25 minutes

Kitchen Tip

This dish is delicious served topped with shredded reduced-fat Cheddar cheese.

¾ pound ground beef (85% lean)

1 medium onion, chopped (about ½ cup)

1 tablespoon chili powder

1 can (10¾ ounces) Campbell's® Healthy Request® Condensed Tomato Soup

¼ cup water

1 teaspoon vinegar

1 can (about 15 ounces) kidney beans, rinsed and drained

4 cups hot cooked regular long-grain white rice, cooked without salt

1. Cook the beef, onion and chili powder in a 10-inch skillet over medium-high heat until the beef is well browned, stirring often. Pour off any fat.

2. Stir the soup, water, vinegar and beans in the skillet and heat to a boil. Reduce the heat to low. Cook for 10 minutes or until the mixture is hot and bubbling. Serve the beef mixture over the rice.

Beef and Brew Stew

Makes 8 servings

PREP TIME
20 minutes

COOK TIME
40 minutes

BAKE TIME
2 hours

3 tablespoons vegetable oil

3 pounds boneless beef chuck roasts, cut into 1-inch pieces

2 large onions, sliced (about 2 cups)

2 cloves garlic, minced

2 cans (10¾ ounces *each*) Campbell's® Condensed Golden Mushroom Soup

2 cans (10½ ounces *each*) Campbell's® Condensed French Onion Soup

1 bottle (12 fluid ounces) dark beer *or* stout

1 tablespoon packed brown sugar

1 tablespoon cider vinegar

½ teaspoon dried thyme leaves, crushed

1 bay leaf

2 cups fresh *or* frozen whole baby carrots

Egg noodles, cooked, drained and buttered

1. Heat **1 tablespoon oil** in an oven-safe 6-quart saucepot over medium-high heat. Add the beef in 3 batches and cook until it's well browned, stirring often, adding an additional **1 tablespoon** oil as needed during cooking. Remove the beef from the saucepot. Pour off any fat.

2. Heat the remaining oil in the saucepot over medium heat. Add the onions and garlic and cook until the onions are tender.

3. Stir the soups, beer, brown sugar, vinegar, thyme, bay leaf and carrots in the saucepot and heat to a boil. Cover the saucepot.

4. Bake at 300°F. for 2 hours or until the beef is fork-tender. Discard the bay leaf. Serve the beef mixture over the noodles.

Spicy Mexican Minestrone Stew

Makes 6 servings

PREP TIME
15 minutes

COOK TIME
35 minutes

Kitchen **Tips**

Substitute
1 can *(about 16 ounces) cut green beans, drained for the frozen. For quicker preparation, omit the first step and cook the sausage over medium-high heat until it's well browned, stirring often to separate the meat. Leave the sausage in the skillet and pour off any fat. Proceed with the remainder of the recipe as directed.*

½ pound sweet Italian pork sausage, casing removed

2 teaspoons vegetable oil

1¾ cups Swanson® Beef Stock

1 can (14.5 ounces) whole peeled tomatoes, cut up

1½ cups Pace® Picante Sauce

¼ teaspoon garlic powder ***or*** 1 clove garlic, minced

1 cup ***uncooked*** medium shell-shaped pasta

1 package (about 10 ounces) frozen cut green beans, thawed (about 2 cups)

1 can (about 15 ounces) kidney beans, rinsed and drained

Shredded Monterey Jack cheese ***or*** mozzarella cheese

1. Shape the sausage firmly into ½-inch meatballs.

2. Heat the oil in a 4-quart saucepan over medium-high heat. Add the meatballs and cook until they're well browned. Remove the meatballs from the saucepan. Pour off any fat.

3. Add the stock, tomatoes, picante sauce and garlic powder to the saucepan and heat to a boil. Stir in the pasta. Return the meatballs to the saucepan. Reduce the heat to low. Cover and cook for 10 minutes, stirring often.

4. Stir in the green beans and kidney beans. Cook for 10 minutes or until the meatballs are cooked through and the pasta is tender, stirring occasionally. Sprinkle with the cheese before serving, if desired.

Chicken Corn Chowder

Makes 4 servings

PREP TIME
10 minutes

COOK TIME
5 minutes

Kitchen **Tip**

Substitute Campbell's® Condensed Cream of Chicken Soup for the Cream of Celery.

1 can (10¾ ounces) Campbell's® Condensed Cream of Celery Soup (Regular *or* 98% Fat Free)

1 soup can milk

½ cup Pace® Picante Sauce

1 can (about 8 ounces) whole kernel corn, drained

1 cup cubed cooked chicken *or* turkey

4 slices bacon, cooked and crumbled

  Shredded Cheddar cheese

  Sliced green onion

1. Heat the soup, milk, picante sauce, corn, chicken and bacon in a 3-quart saucepan over medium heat until the mixture is hot and bubbling, stirring occasionally.

2. Sprinkle with the cheese and onion. Drizzle **each** serving with additional picante sauce.

Hearty Vegetarian Chili

Makes 4 servings

PREP TIME
10 minutes

COOK TIME
20 minutes

2 tablespoons vegetable oil

1 large onion, chopped (about 1 cup)

1 small green pepper, chopped (about ½ cup)

¼ teaspoon garlic powder *or* 2 small garlic cloves, minced

1 tablespoon chili powder

½ teaspoon ground cumin

2½ cups V8® 100% Vegetable Juice

1 can (about 15 ounces) black beans *or* red kidney beans, rinsed and drained

1 can (about 15 ounces) pinto beans, rinsed and drained

1. Heat the oil in a 2-quart saucepan over medium heat. Add the onion, pepper, garlic powder, chili powder and cumin and cook until the vegetables are tender, stirring occasionally.

2. Stir the vegetable juice in the saucepan and heat to a boil. Reduce the heat to low. Cook for 5 minutes.

3. Stir in the beans and cook until the mixture is hot and bubbling.

Chicken Soup with Matzo Balls

Makes 6 servings

PREP TIME
20 minutes

CHILL TIME
2 hours

COOK TIME
45 minutes

4 large eggs

¼ cup olive oil

10 cups Swanson® Natural Goodness® Chicken Broth

1 cup matzo meal

3 tablespoons chopped fresh dill weed *or* parsley *or* ⅛ teaspoon ground ginger (optional)

1. Stir the eggs and the olive oil in a large bowl with a whisk until they're foamy. Stir in **3 tablespoons** of the broth. Stir in the matzo meal and any of the optional seasonings. Cover the bowl and refrigerate for 2 hours.

2. Heat **4 quarts** of water in a 6-quart saucepot over high heat to a boil. Shape the batter into 1-inch balls. Stir the matzo balls into the boiling water. Reduce the heat to low. Cover the saucepot and cook for 35 to 45 minutes or until they're cooked through. Remove the matzo balls from the saucepot and set them aside.

3. Heat the **remaining** broth in a 6-quart saucepot over medium-high heat to a boil. Stir the matzo balls in the saucepot. Reduce the heat to low and cook until they're heated through. Serve in **6** shallow bowls.

Kitchen Tip

To keep the matzo balls light and fluffy, remember not to lift the lid during the first 30 to 35 minutes of cooking.

Southwestern Black Bean Soup

Makes 4 servings

PREP TIME
5 minutes

COOK TIME
10 minutes

1 can (10¼ ounces) Campbell's® Beef Gravy

3 cans (about 15 ounces *each*) black beans, rinsed and drained

1 cup V8® 100% Vegetable Juice

½ cup Pace® Picante Sauce

1 teaspoon ground cumin

¼ cup sour cream

¼ cup shredded Cheddar cheese

1. Place the gravy and **1 can** beans into a blender. Cover and blend until the mixture is smooth. Pour the gravy mixture into a 3-quart saucepan.

2. Stir the remaining beans, vegetable juice, picante sauce and cumin in the saucepan and heat to a boil. Reduce the heat to low. Cover and cook for 5 minutes. Serve with the sour cream and cheese.

Shortcut Beef Stew

Makes 4 servings

PREP TIME
5 minutes

COOK TIME
25 minutes

Kitchen **Tips**

Substitute

5 cups *frozen*

vegetables

(carrots, small

whole onions,

cut green beans,

cauliflower,

zucchini, peas

or *lima beans)*

for the frozen

vegetables for

stew.

Substitute

Campbell's®

Condensed

Beefy

Mushroom Soup

for the French

Onion Soup.

1 tablespoon vegetable oil

1 boneless beef sirloin steak, ¾-inch thick (about 1 pound), cut into 1-inch pieces

1 can (10¾ ounces) Campbell's® Condensed Tomato Soup

1 can (10½ ounces) Campbell's® Condensed French Onion Soup

1 tablespoon Worcestershire sauce

1 bag (24 ounces) frozen vegetables for stew (potatoes, carrots, celery)

1. Heat the oil in a 10-inch skillet over medium-high heat. Add the beef and cook until it's well browned, stirring often. Pour off any fat.

2. Stir the soups, Worcestershire and vegetables in the skillet and heat to a boil. Reduce the heat to low. Cover and cook for 10 minutes or until the beef is cooked through and the vegetables are tender.

Chicken Noodle & Vegetable Soup

Makes 6 servings

PREP TIME
5 minutes

COOK TIME
20 minutes

6 cups Swanson® Chicken Broth (Regular, Natural Goodness® *or* Certified Organic)

1 teaspoon onion powder

½ teaspoon dried basil leaves, crushed

¼ teaspoon garlic powder

1 package (about 9 ounces) frozen mixed vegetables

1 cup *uncooked* medium egg noodles

Stir the broth, onion powder, basil, garlic powder and vegetables in a 3-quart saucepan. Heat to a boil over medium-high heat. Stir in the noodles. Cook for 5 minutes or until the noodles are done.

Savory Vegetable Beef Soup

Makes 6 servings

PREP TIME
10 minutes

COOK TIME
20 minutes

1¾ cups Swanson® Beef Broth (Regular, Lower Sodium *or* Certified Organic)

2 medium potatoes, cut into cubes

1 cup cubed cooked beef

3 cups V8® 100% Vegetable Juice

1 can (about 8 ounces) whole peeled tomatoes, cut up

1 bag (16 ounces) frozen mixed vegetables

¼ teaspoon dried thyme leaves, crushed

⅛ teaspoon ground black pepper

1. Place the broth and potatoes in a 4-quart saucepan and heat to a boil over medium-high heat. Reduce the heat to low. Cover and cook for 5 minutes or until the potatoes are tender.

2. Stir the beef, vegetable juice, tomatoes, vegetables, thyme and black pepper in the saucepan. Cover and cook for 15 minutes or until the vegetables are tender.

Creamy Southwest Tomato Soup

Makes 6 servings

PREP TIME
5 minutes

COOK TIME
5 minutes

2 cans (10¾ ounces *each*) Campbell's® Condensed Tomato Soup

2 soup cans milk

1 jar (16 ounces) Pace® Picante Sauce

Heat the soup, milk and picante sauce in a 3-quart saucepan over medium heat until the mixture is hot and bubbling.